Just Breathe: Grieving with Grace
ISBN: 978-1-7341346-3-6

LOC Control #: 2019918923

Copyright © Tricia A. Chavis

Publisher and Editor: Fiery Beacon Consulting and Publishing Group

Grace

Grace is a way of being, of how you treat people. In ancient Polynesia, grace was a state of mind where all was in acceptance. When someone is in a true state of grace, they accept that people, things, circumstances just are. They are not to be judged, and therefore, allowed to live. The symbol for grace is a series of wavy lines, such as a wave. Water accepts a pebble and ripples and then becomes calm again. A wave can be designed in many different ways.

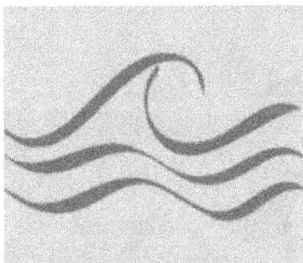

Just Breathe

Grieving With Grace

By Tricia A. Chavis

Thank You……

To God my Father

To my Mom, Dad, Brother and entire family

To my close friends, acquaintances and the love of
my life

To Fiery Beacon Publishing House

Thank you all so much for your love, support,
guidance and prayers.

TABLE OF CONTENTS

Chapter 1

Grieving with Grace

"Grief never ends. But it changes. It's a passage, not a place to stay. Grief is not a sign of weakness, nor a lack of faith. It is the price of love."

-Author Unknown

Time of Death: 10:45 a.m.

These are the words that came out of the medical technician's mouth on the morning of October 13th, 2013. It was a cloudy Sunday morning and the clouds were holding back the rain; my eyes, however, could not hold back the water. My beloved husband was gone. He had complained of not feeling well on that past Thursday. Never in a million years did I see death coming for him! Not now - we had so much planned for our future. Now the future has begun - without him!

What was I supposed to do now? My husband, my lover, my friend, my support, my helpmate was now gone. What do I do? This was the first question that I asked myself. Amongst all of the other questions that were being thrown at me, this question screamed the loudest at me. What was I supposed to do now? Through the tears, through the fears, I had to make a choice. I could either decide to be mad at God for taking my husband away from me or I could choose to be made whole throughout this process. Yes, it was easier to be mad, but I know deep down that I could not do that. I am a believer. I was raised in a household with a mom and dad who loved Jesus. Our home was built upon strong Christian values. When troubles and challenges arose in our house, we immediately turned to God for help. We prayed and worshipped our way through it. So, I leaned back on what I knew. I instantly thought of Job. He is an Old Testament character in the Bible. For those of you who do not know the story of Job, I will give a quick synopsis. Job was a man who loved God and did his very best to live a great life. He was married, had children and servants and was very rich. His job involved raising cattle. In a short period of time, Job's life went topsy-turvy. He lost all of his cattle, all of his servants, and all of his children were killed. You would think that Job would have gotten mad and just cursed God, but he did not; in fact, he did the opposite. He worshipped God! He realized that God does not make a mistake. There is a reason for everything - even if he did not understand it. In chapter two of this book of the Bible, I found a verse that literally carried me through this time. The verse is located in Job 2:10 (NASB):

"Shall we indeed accept good from God and not accept adversity?"

Again, I had to make a decision. Would I be mad about this or be made whole? I made the decision to be made whole. I decided that this season of my life was orchestrated by God. Notice that I used the word "decided" and not the word "understood." I did not yet understand why, however, I had to reason within myself as a faith driven woman. My response had to reflect my beliefs. This was my stance as I

6

began the daunting task of taking care of business. The process had begun.

Even through my grieving, I had to make many important decisions. I began to notice a pattern. Every time someone would ask me about Steve, or if I had to make yet another important decision, I would stop and take a deep breath. It was what I called an "intentional breath." It was a considerable pause. I would literally stop what I was doing or thinking - and breathe! It was my time of inhaling the air of the Holy Spirit. You see, I needed more than physical strength! I needed inner strength that could carry me and support me through one of the most traumatic experiences of my life. This deep breathing helped!!I was approached by many people after Steven's Memorial and Homegoing services. They said that I inspired them. One person in particular told me that I was a great example of how to grieve gracefully. That is how this book was birthed.

In this book, I want to share some thoughts that helped me grieve with grace. The number "5" is the number of grace; therefore, there are 5 chapters in this book. Each chapter holds grace nuggets that not only helped me but can help you as well.

Through it all, I had to remember to breathe. I needed to exhale and keep moving. This is my story but what is your story? Maybe you have lost a spouse (through death, separation, divorce, etc. or another loved one. Maybe you are grieving the loss of a job. Maybe you are grieving over bad situations or decisions that you have made in life. I encourage you to continue to read this book. The words that you are about to read can be life changing for you. Allow the words to wash over your soul and refresh you!

Are you ready to deal with this "new normal?" Take a deep breath!! Now turn the page.

Chapter 2

Releasing the Guilt

Guilt is cancer. Guilt will confine you, torture you, destroy
you as an artist. It's a black wall. It's a thief.

Dave Grohl

I have two things to confess! My first confession is
this: Before I could experience the peace of knowing that
God does not make mistakes, I felt very guilty. I felt that I
was partially to blame for Steven's death! Those minutes
after Steven passed were excruciating! There I was in the
hospital, staring down at the lifeless body of my husband.
All I could do was just stare and think, think and stare. So
many questions were flooding my mind. I then began a
fresh round of tears. I began to feel sadness that maybe I
should have done more? At one point I began to wonder:
What would have happened if I had made him go to the
doctor sooner? Maybe we should have gone to the ER
sooner? Maybe I should have insisted on him talking to me
more? Should I have made the doctors run more tests?
Should I? Maybe I? I wonder if I?

Guilt can be defined as **"a <u>cognitive</u> or an
<u>emotional</u> experience that occurs when a person <u>realizes</u>
or <u>believes</u>—accurately or not—that he or she has
compromised his or her own standards of conduct or has**

violated a <u>moral</u> standard, and bears significant responsibility for that violation." This definition fit me like a glove. I began to feel responsible for Steven's death. Now you may be saying "In chapter one, you were worshipping God; now in this chapter, your story is different." Well, it can be difficult to follow a grieving person. There are so many feelings that were going through my mind. I literally had to give these feelings to God. Yes, this was a part of my process and my processing! I had a moment in which I was feeling remorse. I felt that I did not operate fully in my "wife calling!" I should have done something different. Oh, and once his beloved mother and aunts came to the hospital, I really felt guilty; I had nothing to hide but I felt that I was the cause of all of this.

Guilt can be very paralyzing. Once these thoughts come into your mind, you have to use drastic measures to free yourself of them. Guilt can make your life totally stop. It can bring your grieving to a screaming halt. Guilty feelings can also come about when a person has not done all that they could have done in a given situation. In my situation, I do not fall into that category but for those who do, here are some suggestions that can help you heal or continue the healing process.

This is how I could grieve gracefully:

I rebuked/dismissed the feelings of guilt and remorse.

I had to remind myself that God was in control. I had no power over whether he lived or died. God is sovereign. You also have to believe that. See, when God is in control, He is just that, in control! He is the maker of the heavens and the earth. He created humans and determined a set time for all humans to live; nothing we do or say can change that. We are not in control even though we feel that we should have a say. God has a reason for everything. No, we may not know or understand why, but we have to trust His sovereignty. This helped me breathe. Yes, it still hurt and I still cried but it was with purpose. (We will talk more about crying and tears in the next chapter).

It is time for my second confession! I also grappled with another type of guilt.

As I began to experience life as a widow, I tried to remain stuck in the past.

Let me try to explain. In the days following, I realized that there were certain things that I did not want to do anymore. There were certain television shows that I could not watch anymore. It was not because they reminded me of Steve, but it was because I felt guilty to experience the new shows without him. Sounds crazy? I began the cycle of watching the same movies over and over again. Why? I did not think it was fair for me to experience new stuff without Steve. I played the same CDs over and over again. I was even eating the same foods, that is when I ate (that is another chapter). I just could not bear the thought that I was creating new memories - without him! That was "guilt" talking loud and clear!

Maybe you felt like this or still feel like this. Well, it is so vital that you (and I) release this guilty feeling. Guilt can become like heavy baggage. It will weigh you down and cause needless pain. Also, did you know that when you continue to carry heavy baggage, it causes your body to become unaligned? When your body is out of alignment, it causes other things to go awry. Think about it! You have allowed this heavy weight to cause you to walk with a hump. You are not walking or living in optimal health! It is time for an adjustment. It is time to make a change. It is time to acknowledge the areas in which you are allowing guilt to have power; once these acknowledgements are recognized, then the adjustment can begin. When you visit the chiropractor, he asks you about your activities and what may have caused the pain. Then he asks you to disrobe so that he can get a better look at the problem; this also allows him to be able to see things that you could never see. God has been my chiropractor. I have become "naked" before Him so that He can help me get aligned and cleansed of guilt! He has also allowed me to see and realize things that I never even considered. Then the chiropractor begins his process of pulling and stretching to re-adjust the joints and muscles that are out of alignment. So what does that mean for us readers? It means that God begins to put us in situations and circumstances that will pull and stretch us. We began to experience different and new things. We will have no choice but to act and maneuver in this "new normal." There will be pain and there will be discomfort, however, this pain is only temporary - if you give it some time, the pain will ease and eventually disappear. This is not to suggest that our grief will eventually disappear. I just believe that the pain of it will disappear, but the memory will continue to live on.

When you release a thing, you let it go. It can no longer have a hold on you. This is living optimally! When you let guilt go it no longer has power over you. The necessary adjustments can take place and full alignment can take place. Gary Zukav, a teacher and the author of The Seat of the Soul, wrote a digital article. In this article, he made a profound statement. He said that you cannot give the gifts that your soul wants you to give while you are feeling guilty. What does that mean? It means that you have been left to continue on in this journey called life. You may need to explore a new passion or hobby. You may need to write a book, learn a new skill, etc., however you cannot function in this newness until you release the guilt.

What are you waiting for? In the words of Princess Elsa from the movie, "Frozen"

"It's time to see what I can do
To test the limits and break through
No right, no wrong, no rules for me I'm free!"

Let it go, let it go!"

Holding on to guilt can eat away at you! It can cause a great deal of physical and emotional disease and "dis-ease" in our body. There is no real purpose or reason to hold on to this guilt.

Now, let me speak to those people who feel justified in feeling guilty. The truth of the matter is there is not too much you can do to change the situation. Therefore, the change will have to happen in you! You need to forgive yourself! Holding on will do nothing but keep you weighed down. You will not be able to experience the freedom of living! That is not how you should live your life. You have to learn from your past actions and/or mistakes. You then have to decide to choose a different type of behavior. When you choose to release your guilt, you can cause positive things to happen in your life, yes, even during this traumatic time. I touched on this earlier in the chapter, but repetition is okay. Releasing guilt will make you lighter. It will help you think about more positive things. Maybe you need some other ways to deal with and release this guilt. Maybe you need to go talk to the person-dead or alive. It may help to write out your feelings.

When I think of the word **"release,"** my mind instantly goes to a balloon. When the balloon is released in the air, it goes away-out of sight. I have never seen a balloon come back. It is gone just like that!!!

Let it go!! Let it go!! Your soul will thank you for it later!

Chapter 3

Allowing the Tears

"Tears are nature's lotion for the eyes. The eyes see better
for being washed by them."

Christian Nestell Bovee

This may come as a surprise to many of my close
friends and acquaintances, but I have cried a whole lot
since Steve has transitioned; for those of you who do not
know me as well, you may wonder why I have made this
comment. It just so happened that when I had those heavy
cries, I was always by myself. It is not that I tried to conceal
it, it just happened that way. However, make no mistake
about it, I cried. I cried for many reasons. I cried because I
was going to miss Steve. I cried because I had to now
figure out life by myself. I cried because I knew that our
family and friends were going to be hurt by this. I cried
because I felt a large hole in my heart. I cried and cried.
However, I did reach a point where my reasons for crying
shifted. You see, even through the pain and hurt, I had to
reach for something deeper. Actually, let me be clear. I
reached out for someone, and that someone was God!
Once I did this, my tears took on new meaning. I now cried
because I realized that Steve was in a much better place. I
now cried because I could reflect on eight wonderful years
of marriage! I now cried because, in spite of it all, God still

cared for me! I now cried because I realized that God was still worthy-and I knew that Steve would want me to keep praising and worshipping God. That is what having faith is all about!

Now that's my story, what about yours? Have you allowed your tears to fall?

Tears are cleansing agents. There is a healing that can occur when you give yourself permission to cry! Think about a time in your childhood when you fell and scraped your knee or elbow. Your mom (or dad) probably told you to go to the bathroom so that the bruise could be washed out. After that, the Band-Aid could be applied. Before the ultimate healing could take place, there had to be a washing. Think about it like this: when we cry, God is able to use our tears to wash our spirits and our souls. Then, we must allow Him to put His Band-Aid on us so that we can heal properly! There is sacredness in tears. They are not the mark of weakness but of power. Do you want to get stronger and possess your victory? Allow yourself to cry. Tears are not just salty drops of water. They are liquid signs of strength. They are also signs of courage, strength, and authenticity. What are the natural purposes of tears? Tears clean your eyes every time you blink. Tears keep your eyes moist. This is important for your vision. What do you need to see? It may be that you need to cry a little bit so that your vision (for your life) can be seen. Tears also serve as a release valve for stress, sadness, grief, anxiety, and frustration.

So, what would be the spiritual purposes of tears? Crying can clear your emotions, your soul, and your spirit. It can be a way to purge pent up emotions so that they cannot lodge in your body. There is a healing power in tears. Think about the last time that you had a good old fashioned cry - that kind of cry that has you heaving your shoulders up and down. How did you feel afterwards? I bet that you felt a 100% better! Again, that is the healing power of tears. They are necessary to our life. Did you know that our bodies produce three kinds of tears? Let's explore them now.

Our bodies produce reflex tears, continuous tears, and emotional tears. When our bodies produce reflex tears, it allows the tears to clean out irritants that may have gotten into the eyes. These tears are made up of 98% water. When our bodies produce continuous tears, it allows the tears to flow regularly. This process protects the eyes from infections. They contain antibodies that act as fighting agents. Emotional tears contain stress hormones which are excreted from the body through crying. These types of tears also stimulates the production of endorphins for the body's natural painkillers and "feel good" hormones. Again, we see the importance of allowing the tears to flow.

I am reminded of a story that I read on the Internet. There was a couple who had three children. One child was tragically killed in an accident. As you can imagine, the parents and the remaining siblings were heartbroken. They knew that they would have to continue living, but they knew it would not be easy. Many days after the funeral, the parents would sit around the living room reflecting on the memories of their deceased child. They would immediately begin to cry. One of the other children would come and see their parents crying and would start telling jokes to make them happy again. This became a set pattern. After a while, the mom approached the child. She asked the child why he would keep telling jokes to them. He replied that he did not like to see his parents cry. They had to explain to him that their crying was not exactly sadness. Even though they were sad, they cried because it helped them heal. This story expresses the point that tears are healing. Did you know that not crying (and holding back the tears) can cause unnecessary stress on your body? I have seen many people begin to suffer from body ailments because they would not allow themselves to totally heal. Our bodies were created to self-heal itself. Crying is a mechanism that allows us to rid ourselves of those toxins that are not meant to be contained in the body. Crying is free therapy. You do not want to sit on a doctor's chair and confess all of your hurts? I have a remedy for you. Go somewhere where you can relax and cry!

We are the only creatures that are known to shed emotional tears. I think this is very special and unique. There is no need to feel ashamed when you cry. I had to remind myself of this as I maneuvered through this season of widowhood. This is a unique experience that I am experiencing, and I should reap all of the benefits of it. These are words that I say to you, too! Embrace your uniqueness and cry! Give yourself that leeway to express yourself. Other people may not know what to do with your tears, but it is okay! Let them deal with it! Do not allow yourself to fall bondage to them. People do not understand everything that you are going through. People would love to keep you held hostage to your emotions. Break free from this! Also, do not fall for that myth that says that only weak people cry. On the contrary, it is the strong people that understand the power of crying. They realize that they need to reach to something or someone higher than their own self. So, today, I encourage you to make this the day that you surrender to your emotions and cry! It is so healthy to cry - It is so good for you! It is like a soft, cool refreshing rain after the heat of the day! It was so refreshing for me to cry. Now, do not get me wrong! At the beginning, the tears did not feel like that! They were gut wrenching tears that had me sobbing like I had lost my best friend! Exactly! I had lost my best friend. My eyes remained red for a while; however, I am glad that I have reached the "other side" of crying! I now cry but I remember the good times. I now cry and remind myself that he does not have to worry with the trials of this world! I cry because God counted me worthy to live this life and be able to write this book to encourage others that are on this similar journey with me. I cry because I now know my purpose. It is an exciting purpose! I have now found my passion - the reason why I am still on this earth!

I would like to share a very interesting tidbit that I discovered about tears. In 2010, Rose-Lynn Fisher, a photographer decided to do a study about tears. She caught one of her tears onto a microscopic slide and let it dry. She then viewed it and noticed how it looked. Then she wondered if different types of tears looked different. She gathered hundreds of samples of tears and recognized that the aerial view of the tears resembled the actual situation or emotional terrains. For instance, the picture of the laughing tears consumed the whole picture. The picture of the grieving tears looked like a glass picture that had been shattered into thousands of little pieces. Why would I share this? It further explains why you should permit yourself to cry. You need to breathe. Emotional experiences need to breathe! Your tears are words that your heart cannot express. Again, this is ok! Let your heart breathe! Your heart needs to continue to beat. You have work to do! Do not let your lack of tears bind you up! Be free to do what you need to do!

Chapter 4

Choosing to Live

"Do what makes you happy, be with who makes you smile, laugh as much as you breathe, and love as long as you live."

Rachel Ann Nunes

This chapter begins with my ending in mind. This chapter signifies a choice that I made. When did I make this decision? I had to make this decision on that fateful day in October. Standing over the lifeless body of my husband, I had to make a decision. I could either keep living or I could just allow myself to die. I will confess that it was easier to just give up and die, maybe not physically but more emotionally. I could have retreated into my personal cave coming out whenever I wanted to; yes I could have done that. Yes, I could have "disappeared" into the night. I could have died to my feelings, choosing to be numb and unresponsive. Yes, as I reflect on this, I could have done that! I knew that the choice that I made could affect generations and other people. I had a lot to consider. So, do you know what I did? I took a deep breath and kept right on living. I had to look very hard into my present and near future.

Now I do need to make this statement. My choice to live took on two dimensions. What do you mean by that? I will begin to clarify. In the beginning you see, I chose to live, as in to exist or to continue breathing. However, I realized that God wanted me to live abundantly or live out loud. Let's hash this out.

*Others that need your gift (Unmistakable purpose)

*Untapped potential

*Unexpected blessings

*Unity of oneself (maybe)

As the days began to pass by, I began to question whether I continue to pursue this thing called life or just find an unoccupied hole and join in. I was sure that there would be others there, too. I would not be lonely because as the old saying goes, "misery loves company!" As I said earlier, it would have been very easy to do. Once the funeral was over, my apartment became very quiet. My parents went back to their home, which is an hour and a half away. My friends went back to their everyday lives. Even the funeral home employees took away their chairs and other items that they had left for my use. Once the door closed, it became quiet. It was now just me and my thoughts. See, I had a lot of "thinkers and doers" around me. They thought for me. If I was hungry or thirsty, they immediately met my need. If I needed to make a phone call, they would take the phone and call for me. They were there to make my life easier. So, once they left, I breathed a sigh of relief but realized that - I was all alone. It was now time for me to make my own decisions. It was now time for me to focus on next steps. Doing this would require me to continue living. I promise you it was hard at first. I had those moments where I just wanted to lay in my bed and just let each day sail on by without my participation. Oh how easy it was to have one hand on the remote control and my other hand on a pack of gum! (Chewing gum became a strong addiction for me; I opted to chew gum rather than eat food) Anyway, I digress. It was so easy to let one TV show come on and go off, and then watch the next TV show come on and go off; this was a pattern that I took on as living. This is what I meant by living. It was not really purposeful. I was still breathing and existing but that was about it. I watched each day flow into the next day-again without really participating. I cannot really tell when I had that "AHA" moment. All I know is that it just happened! I had to go through my process. Reader let me encourage you: It is okay to go through your process; it is quite healthy to do this. When my process ended, I had the sudden revelation that I needed to do more with my life. There was a reason that I was still left on this earth. I had to come to the realization that Steve had completed all that he was supposed to do on this earth.

Diana Ross had a hit with a song titled "It's My Turn." Yes, I still have the 45 record at my home. (No, I am not old, just seasoned). The lyrics of this song are very poignant. This song was written for a movie of the same title. The movie was about a woman named Kate. She was a math professor who was living with a man. She was not fully satisfied with her life. She traveled to New York for a job interview. While there, she attended the wedding of her widowed father and met a married man. They developed mutual feelings for each other and eventually had an affair. She goes back to her home state and leaves the man she was living with. She does not know what the future holds for her. Then the song "It's My Turn", by Diana Ross comes on:

I can't cover up my feelings
In the name of love
Or play it safe
For a while that was easy
And if living for myself
Is what I'm guilty of
Go on and sentence me
I'll still be free
It's my turn
To see what I can see
I hope you'll understand
This time's just for me
Because it's my turn
With no apologies
I've given up the truth
To those I've tried to please
But now it's my turn
If I don't have all the answers
At least I know I'll take my share of chances
Ain't no use of holding on
When nothing stays the same
So I'll let it rain
'Cause the rain ain't gonna hurt me
And I'll let you go
'Though I know it won't be easy
It's my turn
With no more room for lies
For years I'd seen my life
Through someone else's eyes
And now it's my turn
To try and find my way

And if I should get lost
At least I'll own today
It's my turn
Yes, it's my turn
And there ain't no use in holding on
When nothing stays the same
So I'll let it rain
'Cause the rain ain't gonna hurt me
And I'll let you go
'Though I know it won't be easy
It's my turn
To see what I can see
I hope you'll understand
This time's just for me
Because it's my turn
To turn and say good-bye
I sure would like to know
That you're still on my side
Because it's my turn
It's my turn
It's my turn
To start from number one
Trying to undo
Some damage that's been done
But now it's my turn
To reach and touch the sky
No one's gonna say
At least I didn't try

As I read these lyrics, my eyes began to fill with tears. This song spoke volumes to my current state of living. I had to decree and declare that it was now my turn. I had to choose to live! Let me clarify further. I was a dedicated wife to my husband. I put his needs before mine. I made sure that he was taking care of daily-even though I was the spoiled one! I even put some of my dreams and aspirations on hold just so that I could "promote" my husband. No, I was not bitter about this; I just became complacent. I began to settle. Now that I can look back on these last eight years, I realize that I had settled. I forgot what it meant to fight for my dreams. There were many gifts that were dormant in me. So now I hope that you are beginning to understand - I had to choose life!

What is inside of you that needs to live? No matter what or who has died in your life, today the call is for you to accept the challenge to choose to live!! Why? Because there is

*Unmistakable purpose in you

*Untapped potential in you

*Unexpected blessings for you

What has God called you to do on this earth? Could it be that you are still left on this earth to fulfill a purpose and/or destiny in your life? There are people that are awaiting your arrival. I finally realized this and I knew that I had to choose to live. I could not afford to die. There was still some singing that I had to do. There was still some motivational speaking that I had to do. I discovered that this purpose was always locked inside of me. I allowed life's decisions to keep me "in bondage." I could not deny it. These gifts were on the inside of me and I knew that it was time to come forward. Reader, I would like to suggest that there are things on the inside of you that need to come forth. These things may have been overlooked but now they have risen to the forefront. Come on Reader! Don't die now; someone needs your purpose. There could also be untapped potential on the inside of you. There is a saying that you do not know what is inside of a person until you cut them open. There is another saying that says that you do not know what you are made of until things happen. I can attest that both of these statements have truth to them.

There were certain giftings that I did not realize I had until after Steve was gone. It is so amazing that these gifts would come forth now. I now have a chance to focus on myself - to reintroduce myself to myself. Does that make sense? This season should be one of reintroduction. That is all a part of choosing to live! You have to recognize that your life is really worth living! Allow your untapped potential to be tapped and to be used - it cannot be wasted. There is another saying that the cemetery is filled with unused potential – do not let that be your lasting testimony! Choose to live! Tap into that potential that is on the inside of you! Choosing to live out loud can yield unexpected blessings! It would take the remainder of this book to share with you all of the blessings that I have received since I have chosen to live. Some of these blessings are relational. I have made new acquaintances. I have grown closer to some of my relatives. Some of these blessings are monetary. God has blessed me with provision. Some blessings are emotional blessings. What is that? God has kept my mind and has helped me to heal from what I have experienced. Then some of these blessings are unexpected. Who would think that I could be ecstatic about life after what has happened? This is what choosing to live means! It means to take the good and the not so good and make it work. It means making lemonade out of lemons. It means staying here on this earth and fulfilling your destiny in spite of!

My dear reader, you can do it! I admonish you to choose to live today. Take that deep breath! Come on! You can do it! Go out there and live, live live!!!!!

Chapter 5

Entering the New

"Entrances into new seasons must be preceded by exits
from old ones."

Dr. Henry Cloud

So, here we are. This is it. The new season has been
peeking its head around the corner. It is ready to invade our
lives. We do not know what to do because it is new! It has
never been seen before. It has never been experienced
before and we do not know what to do. It is ok. It is time to
embrace it and move forward. Yes, those are easy words to
type, but to actually do it, how can this be possible?

What is an entrance? It is defined as: a door, passage, or
gate that allows access to a place. What place or places is it
time for you (for us) to walk through?

To embrace:

It means to hold on to something dearly-and not letting go!
That is one definition, but I would like to focus on this next
definition - it means to accept and/or support (a belief,
theory, or change) willingly and enthusiastically! I had to
come to grips with the fact that Steve was not coming back!
So, now I had to make the choice to keep moving on with
life! Life, in itself did not change - circumstances did. How
do you move on? It is done by taking one step and one

moment at a time. It means walking on a path that you have never walked on. It means becoming a trailblazer. It means tossing away the old and grabbing on to the new. It means taking a chance.

Old is just that, old. It is time for new.

It is understandable. It is easy to say but it is another thing to do! How do you move on? How do you begin again? It takes an act of faith. The Bible describes faith as:

"the substance of things hoped for and the evidence of things not seen."

Hebrews 12:1

Practically speaking, you have to get out there and open your heart. Yes, it has been hurt and bruised. Time has allowed it to heal, now get out there. You will never know what is out there until you move. Move is an action word. It takes determination and will power to move. Stop allowing yourself to be stuck and immobilized. There is so much out there for you. There are so many stories about individuals who entered their destiny by moving-becoming unstuck. They did not allow their inner voices to delay their outer movements. What's hindering you? Are you scared? Use that feeling to launch out into new waters. What are you sensing? Go for it. You've been in the wilderness long enough. What is the wilderness? It is the season of your life where there seems to be no direction. It is a time of wandering and wondering, however, it is actually needful time – a time where you get to know yourself. There is no one to distract or help you. You do not know where you are going so you have to depend on God to help you. There is no set time. It could last minutes, days, months, and years. It is a time of processing and being processed.

This last chapter has been the hardest to write. Why? Because it is a sign that I am moving on. I am writing about my future while living in the present. So the words in this chapter are literally matching my life right now. How do you write about what is going to happen while you are waiting for it to happen? It is called faith. The Bible defines it as the substance of things hoped for and the evidence of things not seen. If you can see something, then you do not need faith to believe it. It is already substance; you can see, feel, and taste it. This is all about reaching for what is not known. Martin Luther King, Jr. once quoted that faith is taking the first step even when you do not see the whole staircase. What does that mean in practical terms? Embrace this new season. Accept this new season. Begin to find yourself. Go on that first date. Write that book. Go ahead and live again. Book that trip. Do something different.You are left here for a reason. Seek out the new thing. Don't allow life's circumstances to drown you.

*Before you can truly embrace this chapter, you must have gone the process. Everyone's process is different.

This is the culmination of it all. Decide to live again. This does not mean that you are suicidal. It means that you must make the physical decision to not let life pass you by. You do not have to sit around and be complacent. Get up! If may take a little longer but get up. No more being stuck. Get out there and make it happen!

Your new love is waiting on you. Declare and decree that you are going to be ok! You are going to make it! Better days are ahead! Say it! Frame your world with your words of positivity! What do you want to happen? See it and speak it.

**Starting over again can be quite daunting. How do you begin? What is the first step? The first step is taking the first step! Funny hmmm? But it is true. I think about Steve. I know that he would want me to be happy! He would want me to continue on and not stop living. I believe that he would want me to marry again. I know it - but doing it takes a leap of faith. I can now say that I am ready to embrace love - a newness. I have been saying it but I have not been acting like it. It can be daunting to try something new when you are used to the familiar, well, nothing else needs to be said:

"It's not that I don't wanna live...I just don't wanna live like this!"

-Brooklyn Bridge suicide survivor

"Everything happens for a reason!'

"There's a better you in you!"

"Don't fear fear"

"Remember to remember; don't forget to forget!"

Open doors! Fresh and new opportunities!

Your experience is needed to help others!

This new change brings change! Get ready for it. It is necessary; there is more for you to do!! There is a new life waiting for you to attack it! That is what grieving with grace is all about! Standing the test of time while standing!!

As I end this chapter and this book, I would like to share that I have entered into a new season. I am now in a serious relationship with a wonderful man of God. God does not make mistakes. We will not always understand why He does some things. We just have to trust and believe that He has our best interests. He is in control of everything. It may seem chaotic, but it is definitely controlled.

This reminds me of a clothes dryer. Once the dryer is turned on, the clothes immediately begin to be tossed in all types of directions. It looks very busy and wild; however, because the door is closed, the clothes remain in the dryer. The door is controlling their movement. Controlled chaos!

I invite you to join me and enter into this new season. Leave the familiar and begin to embrace the unknown. What's waiting for you??

Let's enter in and find out!!

About the Author

Tricia A. Chavis is a daughter, friend, leader and true servant at heart. Residing in Greensboro, North Carolina, she serves in leadership as the Transportation Director at The Point College Preparatory and Leadership Academy located in Jamestown, North Carolina. Not only does she operate in this role in a spirit of excellence, but this opportunity has also caused her to become a mentor to the children and even family as some call her "Auntie." Chavis is also a worshiper at heart and currently serves as a worship leader at Elim Christian Fellowship also located in Greensboro, North Carolina. In her spare time, she loves to read, sing and travel!

To connect with Author Tricia A. Chavis for

engagement requests please email or call:

fierybeaconcpg@gmail.com

Phone: (302) 404-3973

www.ingramcontent.com/pod-product-compliance
Lightning Source LLC
Chambersburg PA
CBHW060704280326
41933CB00012B/2298